Girl, You Have Purpose

Discover Life's Meaning By Identifying Your Unique Gift

Atoya Follins

Please email abf@atoyafollins.com
for a complimentary
purpose clarity call.

Dedication

To my husband, your actions have allowed me to experience what love really is. Thank you for your patience and the sacrifices that you make for our family. I love you.

To my children, you know the sound of my heartbeat from within. I see God's favor every time I see you. I hope this book serves as a small demonstration that you can be and have anything.

To my dad, mom, and sister, I am because of you.

Copyright © 2020 by Atoya Brown Follins

All rights reserved. This book or any portion thereof may not be reproduced or used in any manner whatsoever without the express written permission of the publisher except for the use of brief quotations in a book review.

"Scripture quotations taken from the New American Standard Bible® (NASB), Copyright © 1960, 1962, 1963, 1968, 1971, 1972, 1973, 1975, 1977, 1995 by The Lockman Foundation Used by permission. www.Lockman.org"

Printed in the United States of America

First Printing, 2020

ISBN 978-0-578-54603-2

www.atoyafollins.com

Table of Contents

Introduction vii

Chapter 1: Searching 1

Chapter 2: Timeframe to Discovery 9

Chapter 3: It's a Win Win 16

Chapter 4: Mindset Maintenance 24

Chapter 5: Positive Outcomes 32

Chapter 6: It's Contagious 39

Chapter 7: Power Statements 45

Chapter 8: It Works If You Work It 49

The Affirmation Cycle: Speak. Believe. Work. Receive. 53

Chapter 9: Let's Get Personal 61

Chapter 10: On The Right Track 69

Chapter 11: Where My Girls At 74

Chapter 12: Divine Ideas 80

Closing 86

Introduction

Revealing your ultimate assignment in life is one of the most intimate revelations that you will ever have. Many of us were never taught how to identify our unique gift nor how to recognize our life's divine assignment. We go through the motions day to day knowing that there is "more," but we have a difficult time understanding exactly what that "more" really is. In an attempt to explain our feelings, we usually describe them as the desire to understand why we are here.

We describe them as the pull to be connected to the innermost parts of our being and to do our work.

If you have ever had these feelings, girl you are not alone! There was a time in my life when I walked many miles in your shoes. I wanted to understand this unexplainable desire for increase just like you. Instead of speaking about these feelings from a place of expectation and clarity, I found myself silencing them with words that were laced with frustration and confusion.

Sounds familiar right?

Revealing your purpose is a journey of self discovery. It requires that you make power statements over your life and be mindful of the impact of your words.

In the pages that follow, I'll be showing you the process to have your words work for you and not against you. I'll demonstrate how what you say can lift the veil that is covering your assignment. You'll see that unbeknownst to you, in some capacity, you are already carrying out the charge that is on your life.

With the turn of each page, I pray that my personal experiences encourage you to love yourself, love your gift, and ultimately love your life.

So relax sis. Let's chat for a while. Prepare to open your mind, mind your thoughts, and have dominion over your words.

CHAPTER 1:

Searching

For quite some time, I was the girl who desperately wanted to identify her purpose. My desire to understand the reason for my existence literally burdened me for years. Confusion, disappointment, and embarrassment were all emotions that I easily felt on any given day. I had no idea why God placed me here, but I was truly eager to find out. I wanted more than anything to identify the gift that had been hand picked just for me. I wanted to serve my assigned tribe and feel as if my life had meaning. Honestly, I wanted to feel necessary. One of the greatest challenges in my pursuit of purpose was what I describe as benign envy. I compared myself to the boss chicks of social media who seemed to have it all figured out. Although happy for what I perceived as them being successful, I wanted to understand my thing, my gift that would make room for me just as they did. I wanted to make money in my sleep, travel the world, and live both a fabulous and fulfilling life. This envy, although innocent in a way, was the culprit of me often having negative thoughts about myself. It led me to believe that the picture perfect influencer photos that I saw on Instagram, Facebook, and other social media sites, were the writings on the wall that I was less than and failing in life. How was I here - now in my thirties with no understanding of my gift?

To answer all of the questions that I had floating around in my pretty little head, I convinced myself that in order to reveal and have the opportunity to freely flow in my purpose, I had to experience a terrible, life altering situation. I felt that all of the women who I admired had a "story." Most of them had devastating experiences such as death, abuse, hitting rock bottom, depression, or maybe even divorce. Surely pain was the sacrifice needed in order to gain clear direction. I now look back and realize that this thought process was insane! How crazy it was for me to believe that God HAD to take me to a very dry place in order to reveal His plans for my life. How crazy it was to compare my real life to the curated content carefully displayed on someone's social media page, and how crazy it was that I had a story, like we all do, that I had not honored.

Purpose can be birthed in pain, but to basically raise your hand and volunteer for it is never necessary! Have you ever thought that you didn't have a story? This may have led you to believe that your life did not have a purpose. GIRL, I'm here to let you know that you have a story, a purpose, and everything in between.

GIRL, YOU HAVE PURPOSE

God's desire is never to sadden you with thoughts of not having or being confused about your ordained assignment.

God never has been and will never be the author of confusion. Purpose is something that cannot be found in the comparison of yourself to others, nor does it have to be revealed by way of hardship. It's such a personal assignment that unless you have a front row seat to the in's and out's of a person's daily life, you will never truly know their struggles when identifying their life's meaning, understanding their gifts, nor will you have the raw and uncut truth about their journey. It is only through prayer, positive self-talk, and making power statements that life's purpose becomes clear.

During the time of my search for meaning, I read countless articles suggesting that speaking with family and friends could be an instrumental step in determining your strengths and more importantly your gift. I took this and ran with it sis! I began sending messages to my closest friends, questioning them on the most valuable things that they thought I had to offer to the world. Their responses were helpful and very eye opening, but the truth of the matter was that none of the things that were told to me were farfetched. They were things that deep inside, I already knew about myself. I recognized that prayer was my first line of defense in unfavorable times and that through this, I'd helped people overcome tough situations such as divorce, financial hardship, and betrayal. I already knew that I was passionate about supporting others in their times of pain or confusion, and that I always encouraged those connected to me to chase their wildest dreams. Uplifting and inspiring others was something that I had innately done for years. I had no idea how impactful it could be to someone's life.

Even though I was able to identify the things that came naturally to me, I didn't understand the necessity of who I was. I never gave any thought to the idea that people reach unparalleled heights when they have someone to help them overcome obstacles, adopt a positive mindset, and help them make desired changes in their lives. Never sleep on the power that you organically possess. Your divine assignment has everything to do with what you already add to the lives of those around you. If you are honest with yourself, you know exactly what it is that nobody can do quite like you. The problem is, you're waiting for someone else to give your gift value. You are waiting for someone to tell you that you have a purpose and or to affirm you. In certain seasons of your life sis, you will be your only cheerleader! Trust that the pearls are already in your court. A lot of your work will simply be figuring out exactly how to use them.

Take a few minutes to reflect on your dominant personality traits.

How have you already used these things to impact the lives of those around you?

Have you intentionally focused your energies in these areas?

If not, how can you start and how may it help others?

These questions will set you on the path to identifying your gift and using it to serve.

Years ago, I bumped into a newly hired co-worker in the ladies room. She didn't know me and I knew nothing of her. What started out as a simple "Hello, how are you?" turned into a thirty minute life changing exchange. Yes, I had work to do and the restroom was not necessarily the place that I expected the opportunity to pour into someone's life, but the energy that I felt in that moment said otherwise! She began to share with me how thankful she was for the opportunity to work and provide for her daughter. She had recently survived a terrible divorce from a man who was repeatedly unfaithful and disrespectful during their marriage. Although excited for her new opportunity, I could still feel the pain of the divorce. My watch said that this wasn't the time to have such an intense conversation, but my heart said to encourage her that all was well. I understood the sanctity of marriage and the expectation that your vows would last forever; however, I needed her to know that in spite of what it felt like or looked like, experiencing a divorce did not mean that all was lost.

At times, you can be so busy doing life that you pay no attention to the opportunities that God has aligned to reveal your gifts. My co-worker and I weren't the only two women who passed each other on this particular day, but we were the only two women in which the energy required an exchange. While in search of your purpose, pay attention to the encounters that you never saw coming. Pay attention to the energies that surround different people, places, and things. Regularly make personal power statements so that you'll have the confidence to walk in your assignment when the opportunity presents. Just like the "meeting" in the ladies room, that gave me the opportunity to pour into the life of my sister at the most random, unforeseen time, know that the thing that you do will always find you and present an opportunity for its use.

GIRL, YOU HAVE PURPOSE

Power Thoughts

Power Thoughts

CHAPTER 2:

Timeframe to Discovery

My sister, Crystal, and I grew up in a two parent, lower middle-class home. There was not an abundance of money, but a whole lot of unspoken love. We weren't really the type of family who sat down and had heart to heart conversations. Most of the lessons we learned were a combination of figuring things out and observing the good, and sometimes the bad, that we saw or experienced. Sure, I was familiar with Proverbs 18:16 that states "A man's gift maketh room for him, and bringeth him before great men," but the real truth is that I had no earthly idea what that meant specifically for MY life! The scripture sounded important, but the actual words didn't mean much to me because I was never told that I was created for a divine purpose. It wasn't until after college that I began to realize that something was missing. I can remember telling my closest friend, Donna, that "this couldn't be it." There was no way you rush through high school and then college only to work, pay bills, and die! I was sad, disappointed, confused. How in the hell could people really be happy if this was all there was to life?

Maybe you can relate and no one ever explained how sweet life could be when you begin to align with the purpose that God placed inside of you. Maybe you have some of the same questions that I did such as am I supposed to roll over and live a subpar life with no meaning, no passion, and no understanding? Do I get comfortable in an unfulfilling place or do I try to figure things out? Am I the only one feeling lost and confused? Is God playing some type of trick on me?

I've now learned that there is no joke being played, and the even better news is that it's not too late to manifest divine clarity for your life. No, you should never get comfortable in a dry place and it's required more than ever that you plant your feet and push through. Your life will change for the better once you open your mind and truly do the inside work. Your best days are ahead of you and your "it" factor is about to be revealed. These are the universe's promises to you, but the question is, do you believe or do you believe enough to work for revelation?

We've seen and heard stories of how some of the most well known celebrities didn't get their big break by the age that society deemed as normal. Tiffany Haddish was in her thirties when she starred in the hit movie, Girls Trip. Samuel L. Jackson was in his fourties when his work with Spike Lee catapulted his career. Taraji P Henson was also a late bloomer based on everyone else's terms. And let's not forget Tyler Perry's story! Do you think that the opinions of others and the timing of their journey stopped them? Absolutely not! The drive and determination that these individuals had could only come with being confident and intentional about walking in their purpose. I would imagine they became laser focused on chasing their dreams. Not because it was some random thing to do, but because they believed in their gifts. They knew the good that was inside of them and didn't stop until they were able to share it with the world. This is just how vicious and eager we should be in our pursuit. We should stop at next to nothing until we are giving all that we know we are supposed to.

Our timing is not always God's timing. He has given each and every one of us a specific assignment and it truly doesn't matter who believes that it's too late to be fulfilled.

At the age of twenty-nine I almost allowed myself to believe that I had missed it. I figured girl if you don't have it all mapped out by now honey it can't be mapped! My most sincere advice to you is to never take this approach! I pinky promise that your life has meaning and it will never EVER be too late. I read a story just the other day about a sixty seven year old woman, JoAni Johnson[1], who had been cast as a runway model. Her face is now being seen all across the world! Ever since I can remember, we're taught to believe that models are typically 18 to early 20's, tall and very slim, but here is a beautiful African American woman who only stands at 5'4 that is breaking the mold. I'm sure her success is something that no one ever saw coming. I absolutely love it! A queen just getting started in her golden years!

> *Even when you believe that time isn't on your side, know that the impact of you operating in your gift will always be the same.*

Growing up in a southern Baptist church, we always had things like vacation bible school and a week of summer revival. Yes girl, we had nightly services for a whole week where you would sit on the moaning bench, seek salvation, and eventually give your life to Christ. The thought actually makes me laugh. The moaning bench, the first pew of the black church that was designated for those who desired to join the church, be filled with the holy-spirit, and later be water baptized - definitely the good old days. There was a

---

1 Channing, H. (2019, May). Rihanna handpicked 67-Year-Old model JoAni Johnson for her Fenty ad campaign. Retrieved from https://www.refinery29.com/en-us/2019/05/233877/rihanna-joani-johnson-fenty

powerhouse preacher who would visit often to deliver the word. The thing about this particular preacher that caught the attention of many was that he was no more than twelve years old! Listen - he preached and knew the word of God better than those who had been of the cloth for years! He had a presence that ministered to the hearts of all both young and old. Now that I look back, one of the most significant things about him was that he had already identified his gift! Here he was dynamic, clear, powerful and walking in his purpose in his preteen years! Right after high school, he went on to attend bible college and is now pastoring his own church and the founder of a phenomenal ministry.

Just as it's never too late to walk in your purpose, it's also never too early. As parents, we should teach our children that they are so important that God made them for a specific reason. Even though there is no set time frame to discovering God's plan for your life, imagine if we had gotten the memo a little earlier. We owe that opportunity to our children. Of course all of them may not figure it all out by the age of twelve, but I believe it's definitely possible, even if it requires having them sit in a designated spot at a designated time like sitting on the moaning bench.

Power Thoughts

Power Thoughts

CHAPTER 3:

It's a Win Win

Years ago my mother's sight began to be distorted. She started out having a slight blur in one of her eyes and her initial thoughts were that she only needed glasses. Little did we know, needing glasses was the least of her concerns. My mother's issues progressed quickly and she completely lost vision in one eye and about 85% in the other. My family and I found ourselves in what felt like a season of rain. My mother was referred to one doctor after the other with no resolve. I'm convinced that none of them even began to understand the magnitude of her issues. After months of being prescribed different glasses, misdiagnosis, and even being ignored, I was literally fed up!

My husband and I went out of the country to celebrate our anniversary and my parents came to my home to watch my son. When we returned, I could feel my mother's heaviness and concerns for the daily loss of her sight. By this time she couldn't see faces. Everyone and everything was a combination of a black spot and a blur. My heart broke for her because I couldn't imagine being able to hear the voices of your loved ones but not be able to see their faces. In the middle of my living room, I laid hands on my mother, I prayed for her and asked God to send the correct diagnosis by the doctor whom He had already assigned to diagnosis the problem and provide the solution.

At this time, only because I had come into a place of confidence in who I was and the purpose that I carried was I able to boldly call forth my mother's healing and uplift her in one of the most trying times of her life. Know that your gift has the ability to move your family from a place of defeat to a place of triumph, and from a place of comfort to a place of overflow. It doesn't matter what you are destined to do in this life, when you plant the seed of purpose in the fertile ground of God's plan for your life, the lives of your loved ones may be the first to bear fruit.

The romantic relationships that we choose for our lives can make or break our future. Let's talk for a brief minute about men. And trust me sis - I know a discussion about men can be a whole book by itself! For now though, let me explain. In my early twenties I formed a soul tie with a man who had the ability to ruin my life. He was everything I wanted and none of what I needed all in the same breath. He was somewhat controlling, narcissistic, and just totally not the energy that I needed for my life, but I couldn't see past the charm, the looks, and the level of attention he gave. I shouldn't have been wooed by the attention though because he gave it to me and everybody else, but I digress. LOL.

It's so funny how we think we're adults just because we reach twenty-one years of age. We can legally buy alcohol and we assume that the privilege comes along with having life all figured out. When we look back though, we realize we were only young adults with so much more to learn. I had no idea how to handle relationships at this time in my life, nor did I have enough sense to run from the obvious signs of a bad connection. From unhealthy disagreements to physical altercations with other women - the man was toxic. You know how we do sis, we give so much for so long that out of pure exhaustion we eventually decide to let it burn. The truth is that it took far too long for me to realize that in order to get to the next level in my life and to identify the work and the man that God had assigned to me - I had to let him go.

> *So often it's the individuals that you are attempting to have as main characters in your life who are blocking your most divine blessing. When you rid yourself of these individuals, you win big, but they win also. By you no longer enabling them and their detrimental behavior, it forces them to grow.*

GIRL, YOU HAVE PURPOSE

At some point, it's required of you to realize that everyone isn't placed in your life to cross the finish line with you. There will be relationships in which the sole purpose is ONLY to grow the both of you. It's impossible to identify your gifts and tap into your purpose all while questioning your value because of a man who doesn't realize he has a star player on his hands. If you find yourself in this type of situation, my advice to you is to think about the desired end result. What you were created to do is bigger than any unhealthy circumstances. Maybe your girlfriends haven't been able to tell you, so I'll do it in love. Let the man go sis so you can begin to walk into your predestined season of wins and in purpose.

Two years ago I formed a women's motivational lifestyle brand, The Work Then Werk Movement. The concept to work then werk started out as a cute hashtag for participants of a twenty-one day health and fitness challenge. As a Beachbody coach, I encouraged members of the group to push through their workouts, put in work, and later celebrate, or werk, by showing off the fruits of their labor. During these challenges, I noticed that my conversations would begin with me explaining how many carbs to eat, but somehow often ended with me explaining how leafy greens helped with emotional and mental issues such as anxiety and depression. It was evident that women not only needed support in reaching their fitness goals, but that they also needed support in simply doing this thing called life. The Work Then Werk Movement teaches women how to face everyday difficulties by encouraging focused, meaningful work with the expectation that a celebration for overcoming will soon follow.

At events hosted for tribe members of The Work Then Werk Movement, one of the easiest, yet most effective things that I encourage women to do is to speak to their higher selves by making positive power statements or affirmations over their lives. As you could imagine, attendees of the events typically range from complete strangers to some of my closest friends. It is always a humbling experience when a stranger in attendance connects to the motivation and encouragement that I deliberately usher into the room. Days, weeks, sometimes even months before - I am already thinking and speaking to the need that someone may have. I am already praying that some aspect of simply being there allows all of us to walk away having gained something that we need for our emotional and mental selves, and that we become more comfortable in speaking life.

There are people who are strategically assigned to your gift. When you operate in your purpose you will impact the lives of many who barely know your name but know your work. They will connect to your energy and you'll be the solution to problems they could have been struggling with for years.

Never be afraid to shine bright! Just as you can change the lives of those connected to you, you can also change the lives of people you would never think are paying attention to you. One encounter with you may be the reason that another woman decides that she will keep going. Imagine that because of you, someone didn't give up. They may have had to rest along their journey, but they kept going. Is that not life's ultimate reward to know that because of you, another woman can?

Power Thoughts

GIRL, YOU HAVE PURPOSE

Power Thoughts

CHAPTER 4:

Mindset Maintenance

When faced with trying times in life, I can remember the people who I felt comfortable sharing my troubles with encouraging me to "stay positive." The confusing thing for me though has always been why they kept telling me to do something but never offered any insight on how to do it! Exactly how do I remain positive? How do I keep an optimistic mindset? Being fed up and not having much direction annoyed the hell out of me, until I realized it was my personal responsibility to figure out that piece of the puzzle and define what "staying positive" really meant. After sitting with this concept for a while, I determined that it's impossible to do without a plan and specific mindset guidelines that address self awareness, personal development, and leading a healthy lifestyle.

Like many moms who have children and work a nine to five, after having my son, I was back to work in six short weeks and thinking that I could do it all. I always wonder who created the U.S. maternity leave policy because it totally sucks. Here I was a first time mom doing my best to return to work and perform as usual, but in case no one noticed, the difference was I now had a precious soul who often kept me up at night. On top of the physical stress of sleep deprivation, I started a new, very demanding job and had totally given up on my fitness routine and taking care of my health. One day while sitting at my desk, the room began to spin. I literally felt like I was on a roller coaster and I couldn't get off the ride. I ended up in an empty office laid out on the floor. A good friend of mine drove me home and I was forced to simply rest. Talk about scary! I was so nervous after that about being alone, driving, and doing simple things like taking a flight of stairs. I had never experienced feeling helpless, but I was exhausted, COMPLETELY worn out.

Mindset maintenance begins and ends with self awareness. Conducting periodic inventory checks of how you're feeling mentally, physically, and emotionally is required in the process of keeping yourself in a positive headspace and discovering your purpose. If you aren't feeling well, your focus will shift. You'll spend more time and energy thinking about how awful you feel and less time gaining clarity on your destiny. If I had slowed down for just a minute, I would have known that I needed to love myself enough to rest. If I had just taken the time to tune in and pay attention to the signs that were clearly there, I would have seen that I was playing a dangerous game that I could not win. Don't play this game with your gift. Don't be so out of touch with yourself that you're unable to see where and how God is guiding you and what He is directing you to do. Don't be so out of touch that it takes God knocking you down in order for you to surrender to His voice. Be attentive. Be alert. Tune in.

The mornings and evenings after work are typically two of the only times that I have alone. The demands of my home life doesn't allow me to sit and watch tv, spend countless hours on the phone, or do anything that is not adding value of some sort. In the mornings I listen to sermons from ministers whom I enjoy and in the evenings I am typically listening to other motivational speakers. These activities are part of my personal development time. I know that some days you feel like you're in a marathon attempting to get things done. I know that with being a wife, mother, employee, business owner, friend, sister, family member and everything in between, it's challenging to consciously decide to pour into yourself, but car time is the perfect opportunity. Doing this has helped me transform my thinking, accept what is, and dream big about what can be.

So easily we forget that our ear and eye gates are sensitive. What you allow in, is what you get out. When you are seeking your purpose, you'll have to put something of value in by regularly engaging in personal development. You'll have to feed your spirit with empowering thoughts and motivational reminders to keep going. Soon, these things will become second nature. You won't have the mental capacity to entertain negativity. With consistent personal development, you'll find that it becomes easier to operate from a place of courage and power. Operating in courage alone will aid you in believing for the revelation of your purpose and obtaining power will be the icing on top.

We can't talk about mindset maintenance without mentioning the benefits of maintaining a healthy lifestyle. Doing so ranges in actions from making sure that you eat to live to developing a fitness routine. I found that during the times in my life when I fell short on my diet or in being active, my mind didn't feel healthy. I lacked focus, didn't gain clarity as easily, and my sleep patterns were usually interrupted. It took some time before I realized that eating healthy and working out weren't just spontaneous occurrences but that both activities were lifestyle changes that had to be adopted on a consistent, day to day basis. Years ago my blood pressure spiked to very high numbers. I was so uneducated when it came to such issues that I immediately thought the worst and went into a state of depression. I lost 20 pounds in one month and spent the majority of my time feeling sorry for myself. My mind was so screwed up that I couldn't see past the diagnosis that the doctor had given me. Whereas having high blood pressure is a very serious issue, it wasn't the end of the world.

In an attempt to lower my numbers, I changed my diet and began to workout more. Slowly I began to feel better, my numbers went down, and I started thinking more clearly. This situation catapulted me into becoming a Beachbody Coach and gave me the opportunity to help hundreds of women change their lives. Coaching then led to me forming a motivational lifestyle brand that supports and helps women live an inspired and faith filled life.

Imagine if my mind had been in a better state right from the start. It's very likely that I would have been prepared to walk in the responsibility of coaching and helping women transform their lives much sooner and on an even broader scale! It wasn't until I began to change my lifestyle was I awarded the blessing of being open, clear, and able to receive.

Although you may not associate mental maintenance with health and fitness, they really go hand and hand. Living a lifestyle where you mind your health and begin to develop a fitness routine allows you to be centered and have the ability to recognize and hear the things concerning your purpose that God is attempting to communicate to you. If you don't have a routine already in place, start slowly. Begin with something you may enjoy like an evening walk with your husband or playing around in the back yard with your kids. You'll be surprised how something so simple can have such huge results.

Power Thoughts

Power Thoughts

CHAPTER 5:

Positive Outcomes

Staying positive no matter what it looks or feels like can greatly affect the outcome of a situation. In most social settings, I use to have the tendency to catch the wall, stay quiet, and fly below the radar. I always questioned if who I was and the encouragement that I gave could sincerely help anyone. I can remember telling myself that although I was passionate about the emotional and mental health of women, being a source of empowerment was not really "a thing". Who would listen to me anyway? I literally talked myself out of believing that an encouraging word or testimony had the ability to be laced in power. As I was laying on my couch one day, I can remember receiving a text message from a friend who was trying to help me figure things out. The message read,"What are you good at?" It almost brought me to tears because at that time I felt like I wasn't good at anything. As a small town, country girl who grew up just above the lower class socioeconomic line, I never thought about being good at anything. I had only thought that life was about survival. I now know that survival is not the goal. God has given us permission to not only survive but THRIVE! It doesn't matter what your past is and at times it's not even about your current! He has placed something so valuable inside of you and it is REQUIRED that you tap into it with positivity and confidence.

No longer do I look to fly below the radar. No longer am I intimidated by being asked what I'm good at. I can boldly say that I change lives! I love women with the heart of God and help them see themselves as God sees them. I think more positively about who I am and what I do. I uplift, motivate, encourage, and inspire instead of thinking that those things have no value. I know that in a world where depression and anxiety are at an all time high, I am necessary and so are you.

Having a positive mindset shifts the atmosphere. It allows you to truly discover life's meaning and it opens doors for the necessary connections to the people, places, and things that God has assigned to your name. Not only does it open the door for you to pour into the lives of others, it also allows you to receive. As for me, yes I change lives, but having the ability to do so changes me for the better. Purpose resides in the positive chambers of your being and there is no way to fully access it unless you start to always see the good. No matter how bad you think your situation may be, someone else may truly have it worse than your mind can comprehend.

There was a time in my life where I barely made it through each day. I was physically exhausted, mentally famished, and soulfully tired. I wanted to gracefully bow out of doing life each day. Why get up and go to work because I hate my job? Why try to make my relationship work because he'll cheat soon? Why talk to my friends because they don't believe in me anyway? I mean I had one negative thought after the other. I was miserable and forcing my negative energy on everyone connected to me. I wanted to live better, but GIRL, I truly did not know how. My mindset was so messed up that I couldn't hear God speaking to me about His plans for my life or about the ways that He would use me and my unique gift. The only thing I knew was that I was brokenhearted, empty. I couldn't believe past my pain. For the lack of a better description, I felt stuck. I didn't know how to turn things around and start being happy again.

So many of us fail to identify when we are in this place and unconsciously may feel as if we don't have the ability to think better. That's a lie! Through mindfulness and being attentive sis, we have the ability to change our thoughts and to focus on the brighter side of things. If anything, and I do mean anything, comes to mind that does not feel like love and light, check it at the door! Dismiss it. Politely put it out of your mind and say out loud "this thought does not belong here." Go ahead. Give it a try. "This thought does not belong here!" Felt amazing right? I knew that it would.

Marriage is a very sensitive subject among women who are older than thirty years old. About this time is when women begin to believe that they will not meet the right man and that they possibly won't get married. There was a very short period of time when I believed the same. I wish I could tell you what changed my thinking, but I really have no idea what it was. One random day, while sitting in my one bedroom apartment, I decided to stop being a negative Nancy when it came to marriage. I started to tell myself that I would get married in a blush wedding dress and that I would have a destination wedding. My husband and I were dating at the time, but weren't anywhere near getting engaged. We weren't even really having the conversation. To seal the deal on my thinking, I opened a bank account just so I could start saving for my blush wedding dress. Every pay period I would have a small amount direct deposited into the account. I didn't share my thoughts with anyone but I knew that one day I would be married. I'm sure I saved up money for about two years. Never once letting my mind fool me into thinking that I was saving in vain.

In doing this I learned that your mindset is so powerful that it has the ability to create your reality. One kid and a few years later, my husband proposed to me. We went on to have the destination wedding that I said I would, and I walked down the aisle in the most beautiful blush dress ever! Just as my mindset manifested the non-traditional wedding that I desired, your thinking has the ability to manifest your purpose. Have the mindset that there is something inside of you that will change lives near and far. Have the mindset that there are people waiting on you to use your gift and that your gift will lead to a more meaningful and purpose driven life.

GIRL, YOU HAVE PURPOSE

Power Thoughts

Power Thoughts

CHAPTER 6:

It's Contagious

Before I realized the unique qualities that God had given me, I had girlfriends who had this thing all figured out. They were excited about doing the things that God had graced them to do and everyday was another opportunity to perfect their gifts, invest in learning, and do it all over again. They were speaking at events, traveling the world, and obtaining financial increase, but most of all they had their minds in a place that birthed their purpose. I was encouraged by their connection to their faith and their confidence in the unique trait that God placed inside of them. Their drive ignited something inside of me that made me feel as if I could no longer afford to not align with the thing that God purposed me to do. Through them, I could see that operating in His assignment was the joy, peace, and the fulfillment that I desired. They never said this, but I had to figure it out in order to sit with them! Girl I wanted to be part of the club! Sure, the material things that they were able to obtain sweetened the deal, but it was the favor that followed their lives by surrendering to His will that I most desired.

> *"Align yourself with people that you can learn from, people who want more out of life, people who are stretching and searching and seeking some higher ground..." Les Brown*

One of the most important things that you can do when attempting to discover your unique gift is to surround yourself with greatness. The conversation is different when you sit with people who are already winning. Vibrations, or the emotional state of others, as well as the priceless knowledge that they may have learned, has the ability to unintentionally cause you to operate at a higher level. They'll see things in you that you don't see in yourself and these things will help you bring forth your purpose. It's impossible to be around someone whose light shines brightly and not be motivated. When you can see the fruit of them understanding their assignment, that same energy will guide you in being committed to understanding yours.

My best friend's mom is hands down the most optimistic person I know. She has looked cancer dead in the face not once, but three times and beat it every time! I can still remember the day that my girlfriend told me about her mother's diagnosis. I was a student worker in the telecommunications department at Mississippi State University and while busy at work, my friend shared the news. My grandfather had previously been diagnosed, so I understood the effect that cancer could have on the body as well as the pain it could cause a family. My girl's mom though, she was something like a soldier! This disease had no chance in hell with her! Her mindset literally healed her. Did she understand the doctor's diagnose? Yes. Did she take their advice and begin the suggested chemotherapy and radiation treatments? Yes, but she trained her mind to believe that she would not be defeated. I can remember laughing every time she bumped into someone who asked her about her illness. She would confess that she didn't have cancer and the authority in her voice could make the demons in hell get in line! You couldn't help but walk away inspired by her faith. She had more life to live and was focused on doing so. Her being sure that she would get through this valley in her life caused me to wholeheartedly believe with her. She completely shifted the way I saw sickness or any other hardship that life could bring. Regardless of the times that I had seen this condition claim the lives of so many people that I loved, this time, I KNEW it had no hold.

When you are connected to a person, you are connected to their mindset. Mrs. Donna first imagined her healing, she believed in her healing, and then by faith she physically received her healing.

Now, imagine what happens when you begin to believe in the plans that God has for your life and you link arms with someone that believes with and for you. Imagine what happens when you are associating with someone who believes that you are amazing and that amazing things will come through you. Imagine what happens when you and those around you only believe the good. These types of shared mindsets are the recipe for your life to have an impact beyond belief.

GIRL, YOU HAVE PURPOSE

Power Thoughts

Power Thoughts

CHAPTER 7:

Power Statements

Power statements are the positive things that we speak over ourselves, speak over our lives, and desire as our truth. Isn't it funny how we can so easily say something good about someone else but have a hard time affirming ourselves. I'm the girl who always praises other women. I mean I will definitely give you all the props when they are justly due; however, there were times when I would struggle when it came to recognizing my good or speaking about the things that I did well. I watched people who were connected to me speak highly of themselves, talk about the things they wanted and acknowledge how qualified they were to receive them, but for some reason, I didn't feel comfortable speaking these same types of things over myself. There is a certain level of modesty that we all should have and then there is doing too much. I did the absolute most! Until I learned better, I greatly confused the idea of affirming myself with the idea of being braggadocious. I didn't think it was necessary to verbally speak about your strength or talk positively about yourself or your purpose. Time revealed that I was terribly wrong.

When spoken and truly believed, making statements of power can be the difference in a life of abundance and clarity versus lack and confusion. These declarative statements are God's FREE tools that have been given to us to exercise power and a certain level of control over our lives. He has literally given us the ability to speak, believe, and receive whatever we put into the atmosphere.

GIRL, YOU HAVE PURPOSE

Power Thoughts

Power Thoughts

CHAPTER 8:

It Works If You Work It

When I first started practicing what I thought was self love and making affirmational statements, I did it with no power, little faith, little to no work to backup the things that I said, and I failed to speak in the present.

Based on my lack of understanding and pure laziness, I would recite a few things that sounded good and then sit back waiting for my life to change and for my purpose to become clear. At this time I wouldn't dare speak these statements aloud. I was uncomfortable and it felt weird listening to my own voice. So to play the pocket and stay in my comfort zone, I would either write or mentally declare my affirmations. I kept this same energy for some time until it dawned on me that my statements were bearing no fruit. Like we all do, instead of evaluating myself and the possibility that the issue was me, I wrote it off and decided that affirmations were pointless and that they really didn't work. God has a strange way of making you reconsider. I started to feel as if everywhere I turned, someone was swearing by the power of the tongue. Personal testimonies of both men and women kept floating around me about the impact that speaking things into existence had in their lives. It made me wonder what I was doing wrong.

There are four main actions that are necessary to take your declarative statements from cute little sayings to gateways that reveal your purpose or that can create an atmosphere to make your words work for you and not against you. It took some time, but I realized that not practicing these key things were hindering me from seeing the manifestation of my words.

GIRL, YOU HAVE PURPOSE

Power Thoughts

Power Thoughts

THE AFFIRMATION CYCLE:

Speak. Believe. Work. Receive.

Speak

The first and most obvious step, yet sometimes the most difficult, is to give your statement voice. Just as I was, you may be hesitant to speak about yourself to yourself, but it is absolutely necessary. Voicing these statements ALOUD over and over again will more effectively speak to and reprogram your subconscious mind. When I reprogrammed my subconscious, I began to process the things that I said as truth. I slowly became comfortable in walking, talking, and showing up as the person that I affirmed myself to be. I began to believe differently and because of that, my confidence was matured. I wasn't so timid when it came to trusting myself nor as hesitant to have faith in the abilities that God had given me.

Girl, use your voice!

Affirm yourself aloud as often as you can. If you're a person who just can't seem to find the time, use any travel time throughout your day. Turn the radio off, put your phone on silent, and speak. The other day I heard a very popular social media influencer say that she tells people all the time that she has multiple personalities because she speaks to herself so often that she needs other versions of herself to talk to. It made me laugh, but I get it. Do you?

Believe:

Have you ever nonchalantly said things that you really wanted to believe but deep down inside your faith was on life support? You may have even needed what you were saying to show up as your truth, but you weren't quite convinced that your words would work for you. This thought process is counterproductive! It's wreaking havoc on the ability of what you want or what you are affirming to actually take place. What you're saying is going forth in doubt and apprehension. It's only fair that the universe delivers back to you in this very same way.

After graduating from Mississippi State University, I ended up back home with my parents and working as an insurance agent. For a few months it was all good - until I realized that the hustle in life is real as hell and that a college degree doesn't guarantee a six figure income. I decided that it was time I left my hometown of Starkville, MS and relocate to an area that could possibly provide more opportunities to secure a better paying job. Before I even had the first interview, I started telling people that I was about to move. How was I so sure? I 110% believed that a move was in my near future. I'm talking way down in my bones I believed. No one could tell me differently because this feeling was like something I had never experienced before.

Work

Now, I've expressed how strong my belief was about this "unknown" move, but imagine what happened when I began to act the part! Let's talk for a minute about the power of not only showing up, but showing up as the best representation of the words you've put into the atmosphere. Relocation was what I hoped for, so I needed to start doing the work and ACTING like someone who was about to move. That meant saving money, not making impulse purchases, getting organized, and mentally preparing myself to be separated from my family and many of my friends.

Acting the part of your affirmation requires that you vibrate on a frequency that will demand the manifestation of your words. Let's say that you decide, "I need to get my finances in order" so you make the declarative statement "I am financially free." If this is really what you want sis, you can't consistently live above your means and have no respect or regard for budgeting. You'll have to put the right amount of grind behind your words to show God that you are not only serious, but also willing to do the necessary work to receive the things that you affirm.

If you are at a point in your life where it is absolutely necessary that you manifest your purpose and live a more meaningful and fulfilling life, you must begin to act the part in all of the affirmed areas of your life. These areas could range from your romantic relationships to your divine assignment. I was once a woman who didn't behave as someone who walked in purpose and understanding of her power, but now that the light bulb has gone off, nothing can dim this shine. It's on girl!

IT IS ON!

Receive

After speaking, believing, and acting the part of your affirmation, sis, it's NOW time to sit back and "watch God move!" You would think that this part would be a breeze right? Finally getting to the point where you receive the very thing you've been hoping for! This step, although last in the process of getting your affirmation to work for you, can oddly be one of the most difficult! Mentally and emotionally we sometimes miss every opportunity to prepare for the things we affirm. Have you ever affirmed that you were beautiful but then when someone actually told you that you were - you'd look around as if they weren't talking to you? I'm guilty of this. For as long as I can remember, I have always had a very narrow frame. I decided that certain clothing didn't look right on me because I wasn't blessed with hips like some of the finer sisters in the world. I'm pretty sure God knew if he blessed me with hips that I probably wouldn't behave. I'm talking about showing them curves off as much as I could. That may or may not have been a joke, but let's continue. When someone complimented me, I couldn't receive it. I typically would respond with a question. You talking to me? Girl really? Like why could I not just say thank you!

This is exactly how we block God when the fruit of our affirmations begin to materialize in reference to our purpose. We're naming and claiming until doors begin to open and people around us start recognizing us for your good. We're not in a place where we can receive all that comes with operating in our gifts because of failure to prepare for the blessing! Position yourself to receive. Tell yourself that you are open and that you have the capacity to receive it all!

To casually think something is one thing, but to boldly speak, visualize, walk in, and expect your Power Statement to show up as truth is the secret sauce. You'll never reveal your life's purpose by only giving a few seconds of your time to what you kind of think or what you kind of affirm for your life. When you can see, feel, and wholeheartedly believe the affirmations that you speak is when the power comes. Become intimate with your words. Feel them, give them energy, and give them sound. This will demand that they manifest. Once I began to put my heart into the things I spoke over my life, once I really believed in who I was and that I had the things that I said, change began to take place. I even changed my mindset to stop speaking to a future place or desire, and I began to speak to the present, to the right now!

GIRL, YOU HAVE PURPOSE

Power Thoughts

Power Thoughts

CHAPTER 9:

Let's Get Personal

I want to share with you a few of the most important power statements that I spoke over my life when I got serious about finding my purpose. When I jumped off the bandwagon of comparison and began to understand the significance of my being, I knew that it was time that I took my rightful place in life. I knew that it was time that I discovered my gift and that I began to serve others in the way that God intended.

Power Statement Number One:

I am woman - the giver of all life. Physically, mentally, and emotionally - everything birthed into this world comes through me.

Have you ever thought about the necessity of women? If not, think about it now. Think about our necessity. Not only do we physically give life, we balance mankind. We're mothers to individuals who never passed through our womb. We're light in the darkest of places. You, myself, and other amazing women are birthing ideas, building businesses, and becoming all out bosses at an alarming rate. Women are love, luxury, beauty, and strength.. We play such a vital role to every moving part of life. God has designed us unlike anything else in this world. We are magical and our specific, supernatural magic will reveal itself and make room for us once we understand the necessity of our being.

Power Statement Number Two:

I am powerful - my presence is enough.

As women, we often relinquish our power by feeling as if we aren't enough. We hand over our strength to the negative chambers of our minds by setting unrealistic expectations for ourselves. Placing too much value on the opinion of others has caused us to feel that simply being present is not enough. We go above and beyond seeking the applause of others or taking extreme measures to make others happy. In doing so, we often lose ourselves. Our hearts and minds are given to the wrong people causing us to make consistent withdrawals from our mental and emotional power bank, but the time is now to change this process. Be intentional on who you allow to be a part of your life. Be conscious of the energy that they bring. 2 Timothy 1:7 gives us all the permission we need to be confident in our strength. "For God has not given us a spirit of fear but of power, love, and a sound mind." Be at peace and walk in the power of being enough.

Power Statement Number Three:

I am open, honest, and transparent.

Has God ever required that you confess a wrongdoing to someone who had no idea of the offense? A few years ago, I found myself so consumed with guilt that I could hardly breathe. I hadn't lied to a dear friend of mine; however, I never shared something that I knew had the power to totally change the trajectory of our relationship. I'm sure you're thinking why open Pandora's box if the person wasn't aware that they had been betrayed. The truth is that when you're seeking divine direction for your life, a different level of honesty is required before you can identify, align, and fully operate in your gift.

You must also operate in a spirit of transparency. Over the years. I have been guilty of hiding parts of me from the people who deserved to know me most. One of the main reasons for this was because there were also things that I was hiding from myself. My transparency to these individuals was more than warranted because I knew that they loved me and wanted the best for my life. I convinced myself, that hiding the most intimate parts of me was protection that positioned me to avoid hurt, pain, or disappointment. This approach was selfish and to some degree manipulative, which is never what I desired to be. Asking someone to show me their hand while only partially revealing my own could never lead to a happy ending. Truly acknowledging who you are, flaws and all, takes a great deal of courage. You'll be forced to face tough questions that may yield less than desirable truths. What if there are qualities that you do not like about yourself? What if you have to make difficult changes in order to operate in God's assignment for your life? What if you have to let go of things or people that you love? It's not often that we commit to engaging in such deep mirror work; however, meditating on the above affirmation helped me become comfortable with peeling back the layers, letting my loved ones in, and most importantly truly seeing myself. I now feel justified to operate as a vessel of encouragement and empowerment to others. If this is you, ask God for discernment and allow those who love you to wholeheartedly know who you are.

Power Statement Number 4:

I am undefeated.

You always learn from your experiences. There has never been a trial, tribulation, hardship, or dry place that you have not come out of. God is so amazing like that. Even during times that the enemy dragged you through the mud - our Heavenly Father used it for your good. Be thankful for the times that you have had to go toe to toe with the enemy. You may have taken a beaten, but you've won every round. You will continue to win no matter what by affirming consistent victory. I often have to remind myself that it's a fixed fight.

Power Statement Number 5:

I am not my past circumstance.

You are a result of all the things that you've been through, the good, the bad, and the ugly. You are not however the negative things that may have happened to you. For example, someone you love may have failed you, but you aren't a failure. You may have experienced disappointment, but you are not a disappointment. I believe that we are guilty of labeling ourselves as the issue versus learning to identify more with a positive and more optimistic mindset. Circumstances are temporary and ever changing. One of the most effective ways to stay encouraged when in the middle of a storm is to remind yourself that it can never rain forever. Visualize yourself flowing and operating as your best self. Show up each and everyday as that person and you'll organically move within your gift.

In retrospect, my relationship with words began when I was about 13 years old.

My dad had a strange way of communicating, and because of that I developed very strong feelings about the way I would allow others to speak to me. In other words, you would have to come correct! Young, old, or anywhere in between, I adopted the stance that you would talk to me like you had sense or not at all. In all of this though, I missed the lesson that although it mattered how I allowed people to talk to me, what mattered the most was how I spoke to myself.

Sis, understand that your words have power beyond belief. Through making your own personal declarations, your discernment will strengthen in regards to seeing yourself and your assignment in the way that God sees you.

GIRL, YOU HAVE PURPOSE

Power Thoughts

Power Thoughts

CHAPTER 10:

On The Right Track

How do I know when I've identified my gift and that I'm placing my energies into the right things?

As I was nearing the end of this book, I scrolled through my Facebook feed while handling my motherly duties, pumping liquid gold for my daughter. While scrolling, I ran across a post in a random group that I belonged to that immediately stopped me in my tracks. In this post, a young lady was questioning how to find her purpose in life and expressing her frustration in trying to figure things out. I found myself reading every single comment from women ages twenty-two through forty-four who either shared her same feelings, had recently obtained a bit of clarity, or who had never given their life's purpose any thought. How ironic is it that here I am writing a book discussing this very issue and I stumble upon unbiased feelings of women from different age groups, different geographical locations, different races, and different circumstances who talk about the need for direction and assistance in living a more fulfilling, purposeful life. The transparency of these women was absolutely amazing!

In this post - God gave confirmation that the work that I am giving in this world to help women unlock their greatness and tap into their assignments is absolutely NECESSARY. He showed me that purpose is a vital part of life that so many desire to understand, and to reveal for their own lives. He'll give this same confirmation to you. Girl START! I know you may be confused, but I also know that if you dig deep, you have some idea of your unique gift. When you begin to honor that, assurance that you're on the right path will come. God will place subtle hints before you in the most random, unexpected places. It doesn't matter if it's a social media post that speaks to you or a physical person who shares something with you, God will hold your hand and let you know that He has you and you're doing the right work!

Picture this, I'm at work completing a time sensitive review when a co-worker of mine stops by to tell me that I have a kindred spirit sister in the building. He is adamant that she and I share the same energy and that we would be great girlfriends if we ever met each other. He even goes the extra mile and decides that to make sure we meet, he'll bring her by my desk. Later that afternoon, he honored his word and introduced me to someone I saw daily, but I never knew her name or her story. After a brief conversation, I learned that we're close in age and indeed do share common interests. She was recently married and enjoys fitness and all things inspirational. She shared with me that she has reached a point in her life where she wants to understand the meaning of it all. She wants to be more fulfilled and sure that she's living the life that was designed just for her. As I'm listening to her speak, I'm smiling at God in the back of my mind. I could 100% relate to her because her feelings were mine yesterday. I mean not literally the day before, but I have been in that space in life where I had to know what and how to live full of passion, full of purpose, full of fulfillment. FULL!

When you are on the right track and acting out the plans that God has for your life, He'll send assurance through people you would never imagine. The coworker who introduced me to my "kindred sister" and I hadn't had a great deal of one-on-one conversations. I've never shared personal feelings with this person nor had I discussed life outside of work with him, yet he was able to see God's purpose within me and the passion within my coworker. When your steps are ordered, confirmation will come in more ways than one.

Power Thoughts

GIRL, YOU HAVE PURPOSE

Power Thoughts

CHAPTER 11:

Where My Girls At

I like to define a "tribe" as a group of baaaaaad chicks who support each other's mission and will dang near push you into your destiny! These are women who are in your corner cheering you on, supporting you when you feel like giving up, and helping you spread your message, product, service, or whatever your gift is to the world. When I first started the Work Then Werk Movement, my tribe was initially my close girlfriends who I knew would support me no matter what I had going on. If I wanted to sell hotdogs they would put on gloves and purchase the open sign as my gift! They would totally be all about whatever vision I had and try to make it work. What happens though, is after you've done your work and become confident in your divine gift, God will shower you with women who 100% connect with your vision. Based on that alone, these women will SHOW UP for you.

For my very FIRST event, I told God that if He brought the support, I would honor everything that He told me to do. When I tell you He favored me! There were amazing women in attendance! In addition to my family and friends, there were attorneys, fitness trainers, educators, financial analysts, singles, moms, wives, and everything in between. The goal of the event was to help them visually demonstrate the vision they had in the areas of their lives that were most important to them. Unlike typical vision parties, God gave me the idea of creating binders verses boards so they could group there plans into sections and continue to add to it as God gave them fresh ideas. I didn't want them to leave and never think about their dreams after that day. The binders provided them that flexibility.

From that day forward, women from so many different walks of life connected to my motivational movement and have reported that because of something that was revealed through me, they have been able to get off the sidelines of their dreams and began to level up in their personal lives as well. If we're honest - to know that someone is backing us drives home God's promise that if you take one step, He'll take two. Show up sis. SHOW UP! He'll send your appointed tribe and He'll continue to deposit ideas that will demonstrate the purpose that He has placed inside of you.

I can remember the very first time that a complete stranger emailed and asked if there was anything that they could do to help me concerning a women's empowerment event that I would be hosting. She explained that she followed my social media Instagram page, loved what I stood for and what I was doing to uplift women, and that she wanted to volunteer her time. Girl what? I sent a message to my friends and asked how I should respond. Why would she want to help me? I'm talking side-eye all day! Guess what? She didn't deserve the side-eye though - I did! Here is a tribe member volunteering to help me carry the torch and I'm so clueless, I didn't even know how to receive it!

Although we don't need the help of others before we start moving, we'll sometimes use that as the reason that we can't begin to do our work. I can remember praying "God if you send help, I'll begin to use my voice, to share my heart in helping women live more inspired lives. I'll show them the things that You have shown me. Yes, I was surrounded by people who would support me but someone who was actually willing to work towards the things that I was passionate about was what I was looking for, and they were nowhere to be found. Your friends, they won't always share your interest. Whereas they are willing to support, they may not be willing to help do the work. It would even be selfish to expect them to place their energies in areas that they aren't interested in, but ooowee when I got busy, He sent all the help I needed.

There are people sitting, waiting to assist you and to lend their expertise. They are waiting to give you the blueprint to the exact thing that you desire to do, but resources aren't just going to reveal themselves. You must first show yourself worthy.

Power Thoughts

GIRL, YOU HAVE PURPOSE

Power Thoughts

CHAPTER 12:

Divine Ideas

So the saying goes that you speak what you seek until you see what you said. I totally agree, but when you are blessed with a divine idea, it's really on and popping! It's almost unreal how clear this type of direction from God is. He will give you SPECIFIC counsel concerning how to use your gift. I have literally been awakened from my sleep with complete, step by step instructions on what to do, how to do it, or who to ask for help. In the event that I told myself that maybe these were just thoughts that I made up, I was quickly corrected over and over again by the way that the thought would never leave my mind. For quite some time I slept with a notebook beside my bed because it was the 3 a.m. ideas that felt the most secure. In fact, it was a 3 a.m. idea that prompted me to write this book. Girl, I almost named the book 3 a.m.! Experience has taught me that God will give you divine ideas, but we can't be timid in carrying out the plan. When God gave me the idea to write, I asked a TON of questions about the request. "God, I'm pregnant. I had a hard time during the early stages of motherhood with my son. You already know sleep deprivation and I are straight up enemies. Are you sure you want me to do this now? Like wouldn't it make more sense when my daughter is about one?" No matter what other times I attempted to tell myself would work best, the directive was NOW!

> Listening to God's direction is one thing, BUT hearing and executing is a totally different animal!

I like to think God uses dreams or the wee hours of the morning to speak to us because it's one of the few times throughout the day in which we are completely STILL. It's during those times when our minds are typically not running one hundred miles a minute and we are in that sweet place to receive true understanding.

There will be many times along the path of uncovering your gift that you will tread lightly and be slow to move on the thoughts or ideas that come to your mind, but there will also be times that will require you to be bold and move expeditiously because these thoughts are designed to move you towards your life's true meaning. It's not a coincidence that you can't stop thinking about the biggest dream that you have. This is a divine deposit girl and it's time to cash out.

As women, it sounds a bit cliche when we talk about the many hats that we wear. In all honesty though, it's beyond truth. Even if you aren't a wife or mother, it still seems that it's in our nature to find something or someone to nurture. In doing so, we'll have a tendency to be on the brink of burnout before we slow down. Can you imagine what this is doing to your mental space? When I thought about how unhealthy this was, I casually said that during mental health awareness month that I would provide an environment where women could learn the importance of self-care from female entrepreneurs whose businesses were based around services that could assist them. You did catch that I "casually said" I would provide this opportunity right? I thought it was just a simple idea that wasn't to be taken too seriously, and that I would get to it whenever I got to it. WRONG! For almost a year and a half this idea came to me at least once a week. I mentioned it to a few people from time to time but never actually put forth much effort to make it happen. While out on maternity leave - I was basically forced to stop dropping the ball. Again, I had a ton of questions just as I did when God told me to write this book, so I made God a counter offer with a time that I thought would work best. I mean geesh - my baby wasn't even a month old! Come on God. Let me live! Needless to say He didn't let up so I got busy and began to plan. His direction wasn't in vain.

All of the entrepreneurs who agreed to share their expertise were looking for ways to develop themselves through overcoming their fear of public speaking. They also wanted to provide more in depth details about their perspective fields and how they cater to the mental maintenance of women. This event gave them that opportunity. Guests who were in attendance were able to leave with actionable game plans to deal with very personal issues in their lives such as infertility and the absence of self confidence. Vendors were able to introduce their businesses to women they may have never met and ultimately increase their bottom line.

What I thought would just be another event ended up being a platform of additional exposure for some and healing for others.

My question to you is, what ideas are you forcing to the back of your mind because they seem to have no significance? What if the execution of this thing that just won't leave you alone will put your life's assignment in plain view? These may not be questions that you typically ask yourself, but I suggest that you jump in and start somewhere. Why not start here? Begin to spend time understanding why you can't seem to get certain ideas out of your mind. The more you dissect these things, the more you'll see that it's all tied to the end result, operating in your gift.

Power Thoughts

GIRL, YOU HAVE PURPOSE

Power Thoughts

Closing

"The things you want are always possible; it is just that the way to get them is not always apparent. The only real obstacle in your path to a fulfilling life is you, and that can be a considerable obstacle because you carry the baggage of insecurities and past experience." Les Brown

The highest and ultimate purpose in all of our lives is to create impact, but when we begin to get into the details of what we possess that will allow us to do so - we find ourselves stuck.

My prayer is that this book inspires you to believe that you are already equipped and that it helps you move forward with living the life that you desire and deserve. You are 1 of 1, and inside of you lies a unique gift that must be given to the world.

Your homework is to adopt three to five power statements for your life. Use the Affirmation Cycle discussed in Chapter

GIRL, YOU HAVE PURPOSE

8 and immediately begin to gain clarity, direction, and insight of your purpose.

Living a life of fulfillment has no respecter of person. You were created with the long game in mind. Revelation of your gift starts now. You got this girl! I'm the friend in the back, the loud one, and I'm cheering for you.

Resources

Chang, Larry, and Roderick Terry. Wisdom for the Soul of Black Folk. Gnosophia, 2007.

Channing, H. (2019, May). *Rihanna handpicked 67-Year-Old model JoAni Johnson for her Fenty ad campaign.* Retrieved from https://www.refinery29.com/en-us/2019/05/233877/rihanna-joani-johnson-fenty

www.ingramcontent.com/pod-product-compliance
Lightning Source LLC
Chambersburg PA
CBHW030224170426
43194CB00007BA/847